D1231810

What Was the Great Depression?

by Janet B. Pascal

illustrated by Dede Putra

Grosset & Dunlap
An Imprint of Penguin Random House

To my grandpa Brenner, who, a few days before the banks failed, brought home all his money hidden in a manila envelope. We never found out why—JBP

Dedicated to my family—DP

GROSSET & DUNLAP
Penguin Young Readers Group
An Imprint of Penguin Random House LLC

The publisher does not have any control over and does not assume any responsibility for author or third-party websites or their content.

Text copyright © 2015 by Janet B. Pascal. Illustrations copyright © 2015 by Penguin Random House LLC. All rights reserved. Published by Grosset & Dunlap, an imprint of Penguin Random House LLC, 345 Hudson Street, New York, New York 10014. GROSSET & DUNLAP is a trademark of Penguin Random House LLC. Printed in the USA.

Library of Congress Cataloging-in-Publication Data is available.

ISBN 978-0-448-48427-3   10 9 8 7 6 5 4 3 2 1

Contents

What Was the Great Depression?

In the fall of 1928, Herbert Hoover, future president of the United States, announced, "We in America today are nearer to the final triumph over poverty than ever before in the history of any land." Most citizens agreed. Life was the best it had ever been. Only 4 percent of the population was unemployed—four out of every one hundred workers.

A little more than a year later, financial panic had taken over. The New York stock market crashed. Millionaires were ruined. Ordinary citizens lost everything.

The crisis spread from the stock market to the rest of the country. Banks and businesses closed. People's life savings disappeared. They lost their jobs and their homes. By 1933, one out of every four Americans was out of work. The crisis soon spread all over the world.

This period is called the Great Depression. It remains the worst financial disaster the modern world has ever known. All the money, goods,

businesses, and workers that make a country run are called its economy. During the Great Depression, the economy broke down almost completely. To those living through it, it seemed like a bad dream that would not end. What had happened? How did the good times end so quickly?

CHAPTER 1
Time to Have Fun

The Roaring Twenties, the New Era, the Jazz Age . . . All the common names for the 1920s tell us that it was an exciting decade to be alive.

The horror of World War I was past. The world was at peace. Everyone was earning money, and it was time to have fun.

Electricity and telephone lines were linking more and more places. Labor-saving devices that made daily life easier were suddenly everywhere. Automobiles were cheap enough that middle-class families could own them. Roads sprang up all over. Suddenly the whole country was open to anyone with a car. People opened their newspapers

every day and saw ads urging them to go out and spend, have fun. Families all over the country enjoyed the same radio shows and movies. Most cities had huge, fancy movie "palaces" where audiences could feel like royalty.

More and more people were moving to the cities. When World War I started, over half of the population in the United States lived in the countryside. By the end of the twenties, nearly six out of every ten people lived in cities.

Prohibition

In 1920, the United States government made it illegal to sell alcoholic drinks. This law was called Prohibition. But it didn't stop people from drinking. During the Roaring Twenties, it became fashionable to go to illegal bars called "speakeasies." People who made or smuggled drinks were called "bootleggers." The power of bootleggers during Prohibition led to the rise of gangster organizations like the Mafia. During the Depression, many people survived by becoming bootleggers. Politicians, such as Franklin Delano Roosevelt, who wanted to end Prohibition were known as "wets."

It was an exciting new time, full of places to go and products to buy. People could pay for things in a new way—easy credit. Before this, most Americans had believed that borrowing money was wrong. In any case, it was hard for anyone who was not rich to get a loan from a bank. But now it became very easy to borrow. People bought fancy new washing machines and vacuum cleaners by putting down a small amount of money. They promised to pay off the rest a little bit every month. The 1920s were the era of "buy now, pay later."

"Buy now, pay later" didn't just apply to radios and vacuum cleaners. People also bought stocks with borrowed money.

Stocks had been around for a long time. Basically they work like this: An investor buys a number of shares in a company such as Microsoft. Now he owns a small part of the company. When it does well, the value of the shares rises.

When it does badly, the shares are worth less. If the company fails, they are worth nothing. The shares' value changes constantly, and shares can be sold at any time for whatever they are worth at that moment. People hoped to discover a company before it was well known. Then they could buy its stock cheaply. If the company became very successful, the value of the shares would shoot up, and a lucky investor could make a fortune.

In the 1920s, the stock market was an exciting place. The value of stocks kept going up and up. It looked like a way of gambling where everybody could win. Even people who didn't know anything about business wanted to try their luck. The most important place where stocks were bought and sold was on Wall Street in New York City.

Wall Street

Wall Street is in downtown Manhattan. It is named for the wall that once stood at the city's northern border. In the late eighteenth century, men started gathering under a tree there to trade. The site became the main business area in the city. In 1903, the New York Stock Exchange was built on the spot. Wealthy men could buy a seat on the Stock Exchange. Only people with a seat were allowed to trade stock. When they traded for other people,

they were called "stockbrokers." Because so much business was done on Wall Street, people started using the name to refer to financial transactions anywhere in America.

When small investors made money in the stock market, they usually bought more stocks, hoping to get even richer. This didn't seem like a risk, because the value of so many stocks kept rising. Even people without money wanted to buy stocks. So they borrowed money. By 1929, almost half of the money loaned by banks was used for buying stocks.

The New York Stock Exchange

The government didn't try to control the stock market. Some economists thought that it should. They warned that things were getting out of hand. People were getting excited and paying more for stocks than they were really worth. Someday prices would fall, and many people would lose a lot of money. But nobody wanted to listen.

Stock prices became so high that they had nothing to do with reality. If people heard that a company was hot, they would snatch up stock without wondering if the company had anything worth selling. Then they would quickly sell it at a higher price. The next buyer would sell it for even more money, and so on. This out-of-control growth is called a bubble. Bubbles don't happen only with stocks. One famous, early bubble involved tulip bulbs in Holland in 1637. People got so excited about tulips that they would pay as much as the value of an entire house for one tulip bulb.

As long as people are eager to buy, the price shoots up without any connection to its real value. The bubble gets bigger and bigger.

The trouble with bubbles is, they burst. Finally the price gets so high that everyone starts to wonder if the item is really worth it. Those who manage to sell in time are okay. But those who don't are left holding something that has become worthless. It is like a game of hot potato.

The Florida Land Bubble

In the 1920s, land developers described Florida as a paradise. Everyone wanted to buy land there. Florida lots became so hot that some were bought and resold ten times in a single day. Some buyers even bought land without seeing it first. Then a huge hurricane hit. Suddenly no one wanted land in Florida anymore. People discovered that they owned lots in a swamp or even underwater. Their money was gone.

CHAPTER 2
The Bubble Bursts

The stock market bubble of 1929 burst with a splat. October 24, 1929, is known as Black Thursday. On that day, stock prices began to fall and kept falling. All at once, everyone wanted to sell their stocks. That made prices fall even further. Prices fell so fast, no one could keep track of them.

A frightened crowd gathered outside Wall Street, the center of the business world. Someone saw a construction worker on top of a tall building.

They thought he was a ruined businessman about to kill himself. Soon false rumors were spreading that hundreds of millionaires who had lost all their money were jumping to their deaths.

The panic ended at noon. A group of important businessmen pooled their money. One of them walked into the stock exchange. In a loud, calm voice, he began buying stocks at high prices. This convinced people that stocks must be safe after all. For a few days prices began rising again, and everyone relaxed.

But the crisis wasn't over. On Monday, prices began to fall even faster. By the morning of Tuesday, October 29, panic had taken over completely. No one even heard the ringing of the bell that announced the opening of Wall Street stock trading. It was drowned out by shouts of "Sell! Sell!" A guard on the floor described the crowd: "They roared like a lot of lions and tigers.

. . . It was like a bunch of crazy men." More shares were sold on that day than ever before. Money was lost with every sale. Millions of dollars simply disappeared.

Stock prices were sent by telegraph around the country on long strips of paper called ticker tape.

The ticker could print 285 words a minute. That day fifteen thousand miles of tape were printed out. But it wasn't enough. The ticker machine fell four hours behind. This meant no one could even find out how much money they had lost.

Telegraphs

A telegraph is a way of sending electric signals over a wire. In America, it was developed by Samuel Morse, starting in 1837. Before the telegraph, it took days for news to get from one part of the country to another. With the telegraph it was possible to send a message almost instantly. During the stock market boom, information about stock prices was sent from Wall Street all over America. It became a popular pastime for people to gather in the local stockbroker's office and watch the value of their stocks going up.

Samuel Morse

October 29, Black Tuesday, was the single worst day in the US economy. But nobody understood what had happened. Famous bankers and businessmen kept telling the public that the worst was over. The economy was still strong and stable.

They were wrong.

After the crash, people began to discover what a fantasy they had been living in. The stock market boom had been hiding the truth. Even during the most exciting times, only a small number of Americans had really been getting richer. The rest had just been spending more money. Two large groups had actually been getting poorer—unskilled factory workers and farmers.

Many had believed in the idea that everyone could be rich. They spent money they didn't have buying things on installments. The gap between the rich and the poor was huge and getting bigger. By 1929, the few richest men in America were wealthier than all the farmers in the country put together.

The idea of ever-better good times had seemed so real. In part this was because there were so many things to buy. Assembly lines made it faster and easier than ever before to produce cheap appliances. Factories were turning out hundreds of radios, vacuum cleaners, washing machines, and especially automobiles. But there weren't enough people to buy them all. American companies were producing more than they could sell.

After the crash, some millionaires did find themselves without a penny. But many had figured out what was going on in time. They saved at least some of their fortune. Those who suffered most were ordinary folks who got carried away. People who had bought stock with borrowed money now discovered what a risk they had taken. The stocks were not worth anything, but they still had to pay back the loans.

Lifestyles of the Very Rich

Not everyone became poor during the Depression. Barbara Hutton, the granddaughter of the founder of Woolworth's department stores, had her debutante ball in 1930 at New York's Ritz-Carlton Hotel. The hotel was decorated to look like a moonlit garden. The flowers alone were rumored to have cost $60,000. Barbara wore a satin dress imported from Paris. Four orchestras played. A thousand guests were served champagne—even though it was illegal because of Prohibition. By the time she was twenty-one, in 1933, Barbara Hutton was worth $50 million.

CHAPTER 3
The Banks Fail

Those people who had stayed out of the stock market now felt rewarded. They hadn't given in to greed, so their money was still safe in the bank. But alas, it wasn't.

The banks were in trouble, too. During the boom years, banks had loaned a lot of money to customers who wanted to buy stocks. Now many people could not pay back the loans. Even worse, many banks had gambled on the stock market themselves and lost.

Banks do not keep most of the money deposited in them. They loan it out to companies who pay interest on it. This is how banks make a profit. But now, rumors were everywhere that the banks had lost all their money by making bad loans. Everyone was afraid their bank was going to fail. So people rushed to take their money out before it was too late.

Huge angry crowds lined up outside the banks. The first customers in line got their money. But too many people wanted their money back at the same time. Soon the banks ran out of the small amount of cash they kept on hand. Then they had to lock their doors until they could get back some of what they had loaned out. But some banks had let too much of their money be invested in stocks that were no longer worth anything. They couldn't get more cash. They had to stay locked for good.

Huge waves of bank failures spread all over the country. By 1933, about eleven thousand banks had failed. That was almost half the banks in the United States. Anyone who had deposited their savings in a bank that closed lost it all.

One of the worst things about the bank failures was the fear that they spread. Even people who hadn't lost money were afraid to use banks anymore. The banks that were still open struggled to survive. They had to demand that loans be repaid. If a person couldn't pay, then the bank seized something valuable he owned. Many people lost their houses or farms this way.

The US economy fell like a house of cards. Each failure made people poorer and more frightened. This made things worse and led to more failures. Even those with money were afraid to spend anything. Suddenly no one was buying all those cars and radios and electric gadgets. So the factories that made them went out of business.

33

Everyone who worked in them lost their jobs. Unemployment went up. Fewer and fewer people had enough to live on.

By 1933, one out of four Americans looking for a job couldn't find one. Among blacks, more than half were unemployed. From the United States the Depression spread to the rest of the world.

CHAPTER 4
Hoovervilles and Hobos

The Depression brought terrible suffering. It was worst for people who had been the poorest to begin with—farmers and factory workers. Many who lost their jobs could find no other work. Some had lost their savings when the banks failed. When they couldn't pay the rent, they were thrown out of their apartments. Those who were able to crowded in with relatives, but many soon found themselves out on the streets.

Rickety shantytowns sprang up in vacant lots to house the thousands of homeless. Shanties were shacks built out of whatever people could find— tar paper, discarded signs, old tires, and scrap metal. None of the shantytowns had electricity or running water. Diseases spread. Most cities

considered the shantytowns health hazards and tried to tear them down. But they sprang up again. The homeless had no place else to go.

Some of the shantytowns were just a few shacks. But some housed several thousand people. The largest ones grew into little cities with

unofficial "mayors." They had rules to help keep
the place clean and safe, and to guard against
fire. Some even had streets with house numbers,
so people could get mail. Most people living in
shantytowns were single men, although some
shacks housed entire families.

These settlements were called "Hoovervilles." This was not a compliment to President Hoover. He kept telling the nation that prosperity was just around the corner. People with no homes were angry at him. They called the newspapers people slept under to keep themselves warm "Hoover blankets." "Hoover leather" referred to the cardboard used to cover the holes in people's shoes. And a "Hoover flag" was a pocket turned inside out to show that the owner didn't have a penny.

For a while the streets of New York City were filled with apple sellers. Apple growers who couldn't get a good price for their crop let homeless men buy boxes of fruit very cheaply. Then the men sold pieces of fruit on the street for a nickel each. In New York City alone, almost six thousand men were selling apples. But very few people could afford to pay even a nickel.

Most cities had ways to help those in need. But charity programs couldn't handle the vast number of hungry people. Desperate men and women did whatever they could to find food. Some Hoovervilles had small vegetable patches. People hunted rabbits, which were known as "Hoover hogs"—the poor man's bacon. (In the South, "Hoover hog" referred to an armadillo.) Lines formed at garbage dumps, waiting for trucks with leftover food

Hoover hog

from restaurants. Mothers sent their children to ring the doorbells of strangers. They hoped whoever answered the door would take pity on starving children and give them something to eat.

Many people turned to breadlines and soup kitchens. These places were run by private charities. One of the first soup kitchens in Chicago was run by Al Capone, the gangster. All over the country, the breadline became a familiar sight. Men stood in lines stretching for blocks. They were waiting for a loaf of bread to bring back home. These men were used to supporting their families. Many were terribly ashamed to be seen in public looking for a handout. But they had no choice. Even worse, the bread sometimes ran out before the end of the line. This was one reason soup was so popular. A soup kitchen could always add more water to stretch the soup further. In New York City, as many as eighty-two thousand meals a day were given out free.

Even during the worst of the Depression, ordinary life did not grind to a halt. Most Americans still lived pretty normal lives. The majority of people still had jobs. Schools, shops, and restaurants still existed. The economy limped along but never completely failed. However, even people who were doing all right were scared. They wore hand-me-down clothes and learned to save used paper and bits of string and to stretch out food by adding cheap fillers.

Free entertainment became an important part of life. Board games, for example, were

very popular. In the 1930s, people started playing Monopoly. In this game, players got to pretend they were rich businessmen. They battled one another to make huge fortunes.

Families would also gather around the radio to listen to soap operas, comedy, and adventure stories. People who could afford it flocked to movies such as *King Kong* and the ones starring Shirley Temple. Movies offered people a cheap vacation from the hardship of their daily lives.

Many men hoped there might be more jobs somewhere else. So they became hobos, traveling around the country looking for jobs. Most traveled by hitching rides on freight trains. This was very dangerous. It was easy to fall under a moving railway car. Since the cars were not heated, hobos sometimes froze to death. The railroad companies hired armed guards, known as bulls, to throw stowaways off the trains.

At least two hundred and fifty thousand
teenagers, some as young as eleven, became
hobos. Many young folks left home so their
families would have one less mouth to feed.
Some were also excited by the idea of adventure.
They quickly found out, life on the road was not
romantic. Teenage hobos were shot at by railroad
bulls, chased out of town, or killed in accidents.
They went for days without food. The great folk

singer Woody Guthrie rode the rails as a teenager. He never forgot the feeling of traveling with so many hungry and desperate people: "We used each other for pillows. I could smell the sour and bitter sweat soaking through my own khaki shirt and britches and the work clothes. . . . We looked like a gang of lost corpses heading back to the boneyard."

Woody Guthrie

Hobos were not bums. They were eager for work. Many followed crops around the country. They arrived in time to harvest whatever was ripe, and left when the harvest was over. But there were so many of them competing for work that they were paid almost nothing.

A helpful community sprang up among the hobos. They set up camps near major rail yards in every city. Anyone who showed up was welcome to stay. Everyone pooled their food. They would throw anything they had into one cooking pot, to make something they called "mulligan stew."

CHAPTER 5
Losing the Farm

In hard times before, farmers had managed better than city dwellers. After all, no matter how bad things got, at least they could feed themselves. But unfortunately, even before the Great Depression began, many American farmers were already in trouble.

During World War I, they had thrived. The government needed the farms to produce enough food to feed soldiers. Many farmhands were off in the army, so farmers bought expensive tractors and harvesters to do the work that men had done before. And they bought more land to raise crops. To pay for this, they took out loans.

Unfortunately, once the war was over, the government was no longer buying a lot of food. Since the farms had been producing more and more every year, suddenly they had more crops than they could sell. This drove food prices down so low that farmers lost money on every sale.

During the Depression, people were starving. Yet on the farms, food was going to waste. Farmers had crops that they could not afford to harvest or sell. So wheat was allowed to rot in the fields. Milk was poured down the drain.

If farmers couldn't repay their loans, the banks took their farms and auctioned them off. In an auction people bid to buy something, and the highest bidder gets the item. American farmers have always had a strong tradition of helping out their neighbors. Now they came up with the idea of the "penny auction."

When someone lost his farm, all the neighbors would gather at the auction. They would not let outsiders bid. Sometimes they even hung a noose from a nearby tree to make sure this message was

clear to the outsiders. Then the neighbors would
bid absurdly low prices. For instance, someone
might buy a cow for five cents. When everything
had been sold, the bank would have earned only a
few dollars. Then the farm's new "owners" would
give everything back to the original farmer.

But as more and more farmers found themselves in trouble, penny auctions became harder to pull off. By 1932, as many as one out of three farmers had lost his farm to the bank.

CHAPTER 6
Roosevelt to the Rescue

It is not really fair to blame President Hoover for causing the Great Depression. He had been in office for less than eight months when the stock market crashed. Still, it was clearly up to him to do something.

But how much should the government do? At that time, most economists—people who study how business works—believed that the government should just stand aside. It was sad that folks were suffering. But if the government tried to fix things, it would only make them worse. The economy needed to be left alone. Then the problems would work themselves out. Some weak or helpless people might not make it. But no government action could really help these people. Government interference would do more harm than good. These economists said the process was painful but necessary.

In some ways, Hoover didn't go along with this belief. It seemed clear to him that some help was needed to set "the machinery of the country" back into action. He asked business leaders to invest in projects that would strengthen the economy. But he didn't think the government should pass laws to control businesses. He expected businessmen to do the right thing on their own.

Hoover believed the government should not give out money in charity. But he did think government could play some role. It could help private charities by giving them good advice. He also funded some public projects that would create jobs. The most important was Hoover Dam on the Colorado River. The Hoover Dam provided electric power and irrigation for the surrounding area.

NEVADA

CARSON
CITY

LAS
VEGAS

LAKE
MEAD

HOOVER
DAM

High scalers at work on
the Hoover Dam

Building it created work for about five thousand people. But around twenty thousand people showed up, hoping to get one of these jobs.

Hoover strongly believed that cutting taxes would help revive the economy. He also arranged for government loans to banks, railroads, and insurance companies. Critics said he was only helping millionaires who already had money.

Hoover was guided by one very strong belief. The government should never offer money directly to people, no matter what. This would take away their independence. It would destroy the spirit that made America great. So he didn't mind using government money to feed starving cattle. That was helping the cattle business. But he said "no" to a plan that would pay to feed starving farm families. That would have been a handout.

Hoover believed it was the job of private charities to give poor people a hand up. In 1931, he announced that the Red Cross was available to help anyone in need. "No one is going hungry and no one need go hungry or cold," he insisted.

He was wrong.

By 1932, about half the country was living in poverty. People were dying of hunger. Private charities couldn't handle a problem this big.

In the Appalachian Mountains, a very poor part of the country, some children ate weeds or chewed on their own hands. A teacher there asked a little girl if she had eaten that day. The child answered, "I can't. It's my sister's turn to eat."

President Hoover was becoming one of the most unpopular men in the country. Up in Albany, the governor of New York was watching closely. His name was Franklin Delano Roosevelt, often known as FDR. Roosevelt believed that the government existed to help everyone who needed it. Before people had lost their jobs, he said, they had contributed to the country. Now the country owed them something in return.

He established an agency in New York State called the Temporary Emergency Relief Administration (TERA). TERA made sure unemployed people had enough money to survive. It also worked to create jobs. It was run by the government, not private charities, and paid for by tax money. Roosevelt wanted to see programs like TERA throughout the United States. So he decided to run for president.

In 1932, another crisis made Hoover even more unpopular. Back in 1924, Congress had voted to pay a bonus to everyone who had fought in World War I. But the bonus would not be paid until 1945. However, the veterans (former soldiers) wanted the bonus money now. In May, more than fifteen thousand veterans, plus their wives and children, marched to Washington. They settled in a huge shantytown and waited to see if the government would agree. It did not. The Senate voted "no" to paying the bonus early.

Everyone was afraid there would be violence after this decision. But the veterans sang a chorus of "America the Beautiful," and returned quietly to their camp.

However, many of them did not leave Washington, even though Hoover said the government would pay for their trips home.

Finally, on July 28, Hoover ordered the police to kick everyone out. Some veterans resisted. Two were shot and killed. Then Hoover sent in the army. Using bayonets, tear gas, and tanks, the army drove the unarmed veterans out and burned their camp to the ground.

When Roosevelt heard the news, he said, "Well, this will elect me."

He was correct. In November of 1932, he was elected president by a huge margin. In a speech, Roosevelt had proclaimed, "I pledge you, I pledge myself, to a new deal for the American people." Now he had to make good on his words.

FDR

Franklin Delano Roosevelt was an unlikely person to become the protector of the poor. He was born in 1882 into a wealthy upper-class family. President Theodore Roosevelt was his fifth cousin. In 1921, he became ill with polio, and his legs were paralyzed. He never walked more than a few steps again and only with heavy metal braces. As much as possible he kept this hidden. He was president for over twelve years, yet he never let himself be seen in public in a wheelchair.

CHAPTER 7
Big Changes

When Roosevelt took office on March 4, 1933, he told the nation there were going to be big changes. The government would do whatever was needed to fix the nation. He was willing to experiment. He brought with him a group of advisers nicknamed the "brain trust."

They came up with all sorts of new ideas. The group included Frances Perkins, his secretary of labor. She was the first woman ever appointed to a US cabinet post.

One of Roosevelt's very first acts was to keep a promise from the campaign. He repealed Prohibition. This didn't end the Depression, but it helped cheer people up. It also proved that FDR meant to keep his promises.

FAREWELL
18TH
AMENDMENT

Will Rogers

In the first one hundred days of Roosevelt's presidency the nation's mood turned around. In less than four months, Congress passed fifteen major bills. This speed was unheard of. Usually there were weeks of arguments before a bill was voted on. A popular comedian Will Rogers remarked, "Congress doesn't pass legislation anymore—they just wave at the bills as they go by."

A FERA training camp

Roosevelt concentrated on what he called the three Rs: Relief, Recovery, and Reform. Relief meant help. It came first. People who were starving or about to lose their homes didn't have time to wait for long-term changes to take effect. Something had to be done right away. "People don't eat in the long run," a member of the brain trust pointed out. "They eat every day."

So many of Roosevelt's projects were known by their initials that they are called the "alphabet agencies." Three of the first relief plans were FERA (the Federal Emergency Relief Agency), CWA (the Civil Works Administration), and CCC (the Civilian Conservation Corps). FERA gave money to people who needed it. It also offered job training and tried to create new jobs. By 1935, FERA had helped more than twenty million workers.

FERA also tried to make use of the crops that were rotting on the farms. It came up with ways to get food to starving people. And it set up the first national system of school lunches.

The CWA created short-term jobs for more than four million workers. These workers built and repaired public structures such as roads, schools, parks, bridges, and outhouses.

The CCC was aimed at young unemployed men like the hobos. The men went to live in camps in the national forests and parks. They planted trees, fought forest fires, and built campgrounds. In the evenings, many earned high-school diplomas.

One of Roosevelt's first acts was to close down all the banks. Then he reopened only the stable ones. This gave consumers faith in the banks. They started using them again.

In his first speech as president, Roosevelt told the American people, "the only thing we have to fear is fear itself." Now he was making them believe it.

Eleanor Roosevelt

Eleanor Roosevelt was a very unusual first lady. She helped her husband with the work of running the country. In the past, first ladies had usually stayed in the background. But Eleanor made speeches pushing her husband's ideas. She also worked for women's rights and racial equality. She had her own popular newspaper column called "My Day."

She received as many as three hundred thousand letters a year from Americans who looked on her as a friend. Many were from children. They asked for a bicycle, a typewriter, money for the doctor, or decent clothing so that they could go to school. Eleanor couldn't answer all these letters personally, but she tried to set up programs that would provide for children and help them stay in school.

The second R stood for Recovery. This referred to laws meant to jump-start the economy. The most important of these created the NRA (National Recovery Administration). It encouraged businesses to agree on a minimum wage, a limit on working hours, and an end to

child labor. Only businesses that joined the NRA could display the NRA Eagle. Most businesses wanted to show they were cooperating. This was one of the first times the American government ever tried to control the relationship between workers and employers.

The AAA (Agricultural Adjustment Act) paid farmers to limit how much food they produced, so it wouldn't go to waste. The HOLC (Home Owners' Loan Corporation) helped keep people from losing their homes.

The TVA (Tennessee Valley Authority) built dams on the Tennessee River, bringing electricity and irrigation to an area which had lacked them. It still exists today.

Roosevelt's final R stood for Reform. These were acts meant to make sure a great depression could never happen again. He tried to control the kind of risks banks were allowed to take. And he made sure that the stock market gave investors complete information. The controls Roosevelt put in place lasted until 1999. Then Congress ended many of them. Some economists think this may have helped cause the financial crisis that shook the United States in 2008.

The sweeping changes Roosevelt made in his

first hundred days were called the New Deal. Almost immediately, they produced a surge of hope. Roosevelt started giving informal "Fireside Chats" on the radio. Many Americans thought of him as a friend who really cared about them.

Since so many people trusted Roosevelt, they started to have faith in the economy again. They were no longer afraid to hire workers or to spend money. Unemployment started to go down.

But after the excitement of the first hundred days, things did not always run smoothly.

The Growth of the Labor Movement

The American labor movement came of age during the Great Depression. Critics said the movement was being run by Communists. Some people even accused President Roosevelt of being one. In 1917, a Communist revolution had overthrown the government of Russia. The Russians claimed that they were putting all the power of government in the hands of the workers. Some people in the American labor movement were inspired by the Communists' ideas. But many were only interested in helping workers who were paid wages too low to live on.

During the Depression, workers banded together into labor unions to give them more bargaining power with their employers. Many strikes took place. This means the workers refused to do their jobs or let anyone else do them. If all the workers agreed to strike, they could shut down a factory until their demands were met. Roosevelt angered rich businessmen by supporting the unions. "If I went to work in a factory the first thing I'd do is join a union," he said.

CHAPTER 8
The Dust Bowl

Even as hope started to grow, a new crisis was beginning. The timing could not have been worse. Since 1930 it had barely rained in the central part of country. Farms there were in trouble. Crops died in the fields. Farm animals that couldn't find enough grass to eat starved. Then came something even worse.

During the boom of the twenties, farmers in the Great Plains had plowed up the grasses to plant crops. This left bare soil. Now the fields were standing empty. With no roots to hold the dry dirt down, it blew away in huge dust storms. Day turned into night. People could barely breathe, even indoors. Cars, houses, and entire farms were buried under huge drifts of sand. After a dust storm, farmland looked as dry and barren as the moon.

In 1935, the farming community had its "black" day, just as the stock market had six years earlier. Sunday, April 14, saw such terrible dust storms that it was called "Black Sunday." The area destroyed by the storms was nicknamed the Dust Bowl. People developed "dust pneumonia" when their lungs filled with dust. Children were lost on the prairies and buried alive in dust. "We live with the dust, eat it, sleep with it," a man wrote. As far away as New York City, the lights sometimes had to be turned on in the middle of the day because the dust was so thick.

Roosevelt's government tried to help recover the land. They stopped farmers from plowing up so much grassland. Millions of bare acres were planted with grass. The CCC planted more than two hundred million trees to act as windbreaks. And the government hired experts to teach the farmers about ways of growing crops that would not harm the soil. Some farmers were unwilling to listen to advice from outsiders. So the government began paying them to try the new methods.

Such efforts did help. But it was too late for many farmers. About one quarter of the farm families in the Dust Bowl lost everything. Many piled into their cars and drove west to California, where there wasn't a drought. There they hoped to find work on farms. Because so many of them came from Oklahoma, they were scornfully known as "Okies"—even if they came from Texas or Arkansas.

They found that there were very few jobs to be had, even in California. And they were not welcome. The migrants had always worked hard. But many people assumed they were bums and despised them. Others resented them for trying to take the few jobs still available. The Los Angeles police chief sent 125 policemen to the California border to turn them away before they could enter the state.

Dorothea Lange

In 1935, photographer Dorothea Lange was hired by one of Roosevelt's alphabet agencies, the Farm Security Administration (FSA). Her job was to photograph migrant workers. Her pictures were offered free to newspapers around the country. She hoped that seeing the misery these people lived in would make the nation more sympathetic. Her most famous photograph is known as "Migrant Mother." It shows a thirty-two-year-old woman with two children, at a camp in California. The woman told Lange she had just sold the tires from her car to get food.

California was suffering from the Depression like every other state. It couldn't deal with all the homeless families showing up every day. Hundreds of eager workers competed for every farming job. This drove wages down so low that nobody could earn enough to live on. The workers followed the harvest from place to place, living in crowded, disease-ridden camps.

The government tried to help. It built thirteen model camps. These camps were clean, with running water, and were managed by those who lived in them. But they could house only a small number of people, and they could not provide jobs. Even as the rest of the country slowly recovered, the migrants remained desperate until the end of the Depression.

CHAPTER 9
More Big Changes

In 1935, Roosevelt began a second wave of reforms. It was meant to lessen the huge gap between the rich and the poor. New laws tried to protect Americans who were old, weak, sick, or out of work. One of the most important was the Social Security Act. It gave workers money after they retired. It also provided money for people who were unemployed or couldn't work, and for widows and orphans. To support his programs, Roosevelt increased income taxes on the richest citizens.

The NLRA (National Labor Relations Act) tried to give workers more power. It guaranteed them the right to join unions and to strike if necessary, and it required employers to bargain with the unions.

A 1935 act created the very successful WPA (Works Progress Administration). This picked up where the CWA left off. Workers were hired to build or restore libraries, highways, post offices, museums, and playgrounds. Many WPA projects are in use today in towns all over the country.

The WPA made a special effort to employ artists, writers, and musicians. WPA murals—paintings on walls—can still be seen in many public buildings. Well-known artists such as Jackson Pollock, Mark Rothko, and Jacob Lawrence worked on WPA projects. The WPA also produced a famous series of guidebooks to each of the US states.

Some people thought Roosevelt was sneaking Communist ideas into the US government. But most of the country was behind him. He easily won reelection in 1936, carrying all but two states. However, the Supreme Court thought that some of what FDR was doing went against the Constitution.

In 1935, the court had ruled against some of Roosevelt's key recovery ideas. This was a huge blow to him. The nine justices of the Supreme Court serve for life, so Roosevelt could not get rid of the ones who disagreed with him. Instead, in 1937, he tried to add more justices. He wanted to pack the court with supporters who would outvote the judges against him.

This time, Roosevelt had gone too far. Congress did not let him pack the court. However, within a few years, several justices retired or died, so Roosevelt was able to fill the court with his allies anyway.

In 1940, Roosevelt ran for a third term. There was no law that said he couldn't, but no president ever had. The Democratic National Convention was held in Chicago. Roosevelt wrote a letter telling the delegates—the people who choose the candidate— that it was up to them. They would decide if he should step aside or not. Suddenly a voice shouted, "We want Roosevelt. The world wants Roosevelt!" He was nominated right away, by a huge majority. (The voice was later discovered to have come from Chicago's Superintendent of Sewers.)

CHAPTER 10
War!

Roosevelt was elected to his third term. He had become president by promising to end the Depression. Things were getting better. But the Depression still wasn't over. However, world events soon kept him from being able to focus only on America's economy.

World War II had begun in Europe in 1939. The Nazis in Germany and their supporters in Italy and Japan were invading other countries. They seemed to be threatening the entire world. Many Americans hoped to stay out of the war. Roosevelt

Nazi leader Adolf Hitler

promised them that he would do everything possible to prevent Americans from having to fight. But he probably realized that America would eventually be drawn into battle.

On December 7, 1941, the Japanese bombed Pearl Harbor in Hawaii, and the United States was forced to declare war.

Roosevelt's plan to end the Depression had always been to create as many jobs as possible. But he had never been able to offer enough jobs for everyone. Now, with the coming of war, unemployment disappeared. More and more men joined the army. Other people were needed to fill their jobs. And a huge number of workers were needed to build ships, airplanes, and weapons to fight the war. Suddenly there were too few workers, not too many.

The Brooklyn Navy Yard built and repaired battleships. It employed more than seventy-five thousand people, working on about 1,500 ships a year.

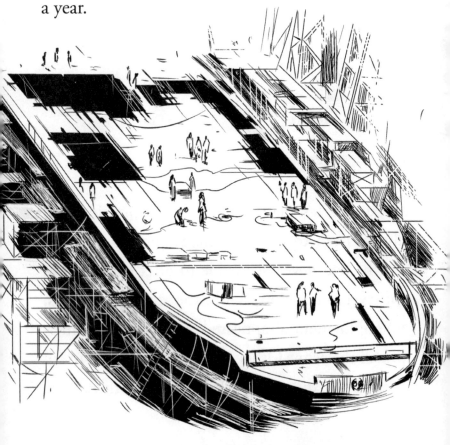

All over the country, places like the Navy Yard in Brooklyn needed as many workers as they could get. They sent out trucks with loudspeakers, telling people to get a job and help out with the war effort. Women and minorities suddenly had new opportunities. They were needed to fill jobs that had not been open to them before the war. Popular posters showed "Rosie the Riveter," a proud female construction worker.

World War II was a terrible time in the world's history, and brought new kinds of suffering unknown in the thirties. But economically, it put an end to the Great Depression. By the time the United States emerged from the war, it had become the richest nation on earth.

CHAPTER 11
The Power of the President

In the years before the war, Roosevelt used more power than any other American president ever had when the country was at peace. In times of war, Congress may vote to give the president extra powers, so he can deal with the crisis. When he was elected, FDR asked Congress to think of the battle against the Great Depression as a war. He needed to be given the kind of power other presidents only had in wartime. He wanted "broad executive power to wage war against the emergency, as great as the power that would be given to me if we were in fact invaded by a foreign foe."

Some historians think FDR went beyond what the Constitution allows. Even some of his supporters have called him a helpful dictator.

The Constitution

(A dictator is a leader of a country who does exactly what he wants without getting approval from anyone else.)

Roosevelt completely changed what the United States expects from the government. Before him, most Americans believed the government had no business getting involved in people's lives. Roosevelt made them think that the government is responsible for making sure all citizens have the basic things they need to survive—like food, education, and a roof over their heads. As the economist Arthur Schlesinger pointed out, it is impossible now to imagine an America that offers no help to Americans who find themselves "through no fault of their own, in economic or social distress."

The Great Depression was one of the worst times in the nation's history. People were afraid the country might collapse. A journalist wondered, "Would it be necessary soon to organize our families against the world, to fight, physically, for food, to keep shelter, to hold possessions?"

Roosevelt realized the huge danger that the country faced. During his first one hundred days in office, a visitor said to him, "Mr. President, if your program succeeds, you'll be the greatest president in American history. If it fails, you will be the worst one."

"If it fails," Roosevelt answered, "I'll be the last one."

Fortunately, that didn't happen.

FDR's Last Days

In 1944, Roosevelt was elected president for a fourth term. He wanted to be sure that when World War II ended, the world would be a safer and more peaceful place. He helped to create the United Nations. This was designed as a meeting place for countries all over the world. They could get together and work out their problems by talking instead of fighting. By then, Roosevelt's health was failing.

Roosevelt only survived for three months of his fourth term. His vice president, Harry Truman, finished the term for him. When FDR died, Americans mourned him as the man who had saved the nation. The *New York Times* wrote, "Men will thank God on their knees a hundred years from now that Franklin D. Roosevelt was in the White House."

Harry Truman won the next election and served as president until 1953.

Harry S. Truman

Timeline of Great Depression

1920	Thirty-eight people die when anarchists bomb Wall Street
1929	In March, Herbert Hoover becomes president
	October 29, the stock market plummets to an all-time low
1930	In a ten-month period, 744 US banks fail
1931	New York Governor Franklin D. Roosevelt creates Temporary Emergency Relief Administration (TERA) to help unemployed workers
1932	In May, thousands of veterans march on Washington demanding bonus pay
	In November, Franklin D. Roosevelt is elected president
1933	Congress passes Roosevelt's New Deal legislation
	In December, Prohibition is repealed
1935	On April 14, the Midwest is hit by the worst dust storms in its history
1936	Roosevelt is reelected to a second term
1937	Civilian Conservation Corps (CCC) is created
1938	A legal minimum wage is established for the first time in the United States
1940	Roosevelt becomes the only US president ever elected to a third term
1941	The Japanese bomb Pearl Harbor. The United States enters World War II the next day
1944	Roosevelt is elected for a fourth term
1945	President Roosevelt dies in office

Timeline of the World

1920	Prohibition begins
1929	First appearance of the comic-strip character Popeye
1931	Empire State Building is completed
1932	First woman elected to US Senate
1933	Hitler becomes Chancellor of Germany
1935	First nighttime major league baseball game is played
1937	In May, the *Hindenburg* crashes in flames in New Jersey
	In July, Amelia Earhart disappears while attempting to fly around the world
	In December, Edward VIII abdicates as king of England in favor of his brother George VI
1938	Ballpoint pen is invented
	In November, Nazis destroy thousands of Jewish homes and businesses during "Kristallnacht"
1939	World War II begins
1940	Winston Churchill becomes prime minister of England
1941	Carving on Mount Rushmore is completed
1944	Mount Vesuvius erupts near Pompeii, Italy
1945	Nazi Germany formally surrenders on VE Day

Bibliography

*Books for young readers

*Freedman, Russell. *Children of the Great Depression*. New York: Clarion Books, 2005.

Galbraith, John Kenneth. *The Great Crash, 1929*. Originally published in 1954. New York: Houghton Mifflin Harcourt, 2009.

Gazit, Chana. "General Article: The Great Depression." *American Experience: Surviving the Dust Bowl*. www.pbs.org/wgbh/americanexperience/features/general-article/dustbowl-great-depression/.

*Schultz, Stanley. *The Great Depression: A Primary Source History*. Milwaukee: Gareth Stevens, 2005.

Terkel, Studs. *Hard Times: An Oral History of the Great Depression*. New York: Pantheon Books, 1970.

Uys, Michael, and Lexy Lovell. "Introduction: Riding the Rails." *American Experience: Riding the Rails*. www.pbs.org/wgbh/americanexperience/features/introduction/rails-introduction/.

Watkins, T. H. *The Great Depression: America in the 1930s*. Boston: Little, Brown, 1993.

A flapper and her partner dancing

Crowds outside the New York Stock Exchange after the crash

Inside the New York Stock Exchange

BROOKLYN DAILY EAGLE
And Complete Long Island News

LATE NEWS
WALL STREET
1:15 PRICES
★ ★

89th YEAR—No. 295.   ★ NEW YORK CITY, THURSDAY, OCTOBER 24, 1929. ★   32 PAGES   THREE CENTS

WALL ST. IN PANIC AS STOCKS CRASH

Attempt Made to Kill Italy's Crown Prince

STOCKS CRASH IN RUSH TO SELL; BILLIONS LOST

ASSASSIN CAUGHT IN BRUSSELS MOB; PRINCE UNHURT

Hollywood Fire Destroys Films Worth Millions

FEAR 52 PERISHED IN LAKE MICHIGAN; FERRY IS MISSING

PIECE OF PLANE LIKE DITEMAN'S IS FOUND AT SEA

High Duty Group Gave $700,000 to Coolidge Drive

Royal Suitor Was About to Lay Wreath on Unknown Soldiers' Tomb.

Consolidated Studios Are Swept by Flames Fatal to One—Master Pictures Burned Include Many New Talkie Productions

Wreckage Picked Up Indicates Craft Went Down With All Aboard.

Black and Orange Wreckage Indicates Daring Flier Went to Death.

Grundy Agrees Rates Went Up Due to His Activities as Propagandist. Favors More Lobbying to 'Carry Out Voters' Wish.'

FOR MORE LOBBYISTS

Morgan, Mitchell Buying Stocks in Effort to Check Rush to Unload.

CARNEGIE CHARGE OF PAID ATHLETES ROUSES COLLEGES

HOOVER'S TRAIN HALTED BY AUTO PLACED ON RAILS

WARDER SOUGHT TO KEEP SEA TRIP SECRET, AID SAYS

SOMERS NAMED AS HEAD OF NEW EXCHANGE BANK

A newspaper headline from the first day of the crash

A ticker-tape machine

President Herbert Hoover

The Hoover Dam and Lake Mead

President and Mrs. Franklin D. Roosevelt

A breadline in New York City

A breadline in Los Angeles

Unemployed men eat bread and soup on a breadline

Homeless men do laundry in a shantytown

Children carry signs at a demonstration for the Workers Alliance

A dust storm hits a town in 1937

A farm in Texas during the Dust Bowl

A woman and her children at a Farm Security Administration cooperative

"Okies" traveling west

Dorothea Lange's famous photo of a migrant mother

Bonus Army protests at the US Capitol

Veterans march in Washington

President Roosevelt
giving a fireside chat

A Franklin Delano
Roosevelt inauguration
badge from 1937

WPA artists work on a mural in New York City in 1935

US Navy ships burning after the Japanese attack on Pearl Harbor